CHAIN REACTI○NS

From Gunpowder to Laser Chemistry

Discovering Chemical Reactions

Andrew Solway

Heinemann
LIBRARY

www.heinemann.co.uk/library

Visit our website to find out more information about Heinemann Library books.

To order:
Phone 44 (0) 1865 888066
Send a fax to 44 (0) 1865 314091
Visit the Heinemann Bookshop at www.heinemann.co.uk/library to browse
our catalogue and order online.

Produced for Heinemann Library by
White-Thomson Publishing Ltd,
Bridgewater Business Centre,
210 High Street,
Lewes, East Sussex BN7 2NH

First published in Great Britain by Heinemann Library,
Jordan Hill, Oxford OX2 8EJ, part of Harcourt Education.

Heinemann Library is a registered trademark of Harcourt
Education Ltd.

Consultant: Ann Fullick, Webucators
Commissioning editors: Andrew Farrow and
    Steve White-Thomson
Editors: Kelly Davis and Richard Woodham
Proofreader: Catherine Clarke
Design: Tim Mayer
Picture research: Amy Sparks
Artwork: William Donohoe

Originated by RMW
Printed and bound in China by Leo Paper Group Ltd

10 digit ISBN 043118660X
13 digit ISBN 978-0-431-18660-3
11 10 09 08 07
10 9 8 7 6 5 4 3 2 1

British Library Cataloguing in Publication Data
Solway, Andrew
From Gunpowder to Laser Chemistry: Discovering
Chemical Reactions
541.3'9

A full catalogue record for this book is available from the
British Library.

Teflon® and Kevlar® are registered trademarks owned
by DuPont Chemicals.

Acknowledgements
The author and publisher would like to thank the
following for allowing their pictures to be reproduced
in this publication: Corbis pp. 5 (Daniel LeClair), 11
(Leonard de Silva), 12 (Bettmann), 13 (Bettmann), 16
(Bettmann), 18 (Bettmann), 20 (The Art Archive), 27
(Lawrence Manning); iStockphoto.com pp. 1 (Shaun
Lowe), 36, 48 (Dale Robins), 51 (Carrie Winegarden),
55 (Shaun Lowe); Science and Society Picture Library/
Science Museum p. 33; Science Photo Library pp. 6,
8 (Crown Copyright/Health and Safety Laboratory),
9, 10, 14 (Charles D. Winters), 19 (Sheila Terry), 21
(Charles D. Winters), 22 (Jean-Loup Charmet), 23
(Charles D. Winters), 30 (Sheila Terry), 32, 34
(Maximilian Stock Ltd), 35 (James Holmes), 38
(Alfred Pasieka), 39 (NIH), 40 (St Mary's Hospital
Medical School), 41 (Kairos, Latin Stock), 42 (Andrew
Lambert Photography), 44 (Professor Peter Fowler),
46 (Russell Kightley), 51 (Alfred Pasieka), 53
(NREL/US Department of Energy), 54 (Delft
University of Technology); Topfoto.co.uk pp. 7, 15,
24 (Topham Picturepoint), 28, 43 (Roger-Viollet), 49.

Cover design by Tim Mayer.

Every effort has been made to contact copyright holders
of any material reproduced in this book. Any omissions
will be rectified in subsequent printings if notice is given
to the publishers.

Contents

Any words appearing in the text in bold, **like this**, are explained in the Glossary.

A big bang

It is the 9th century AD, and the Chinese empire is at the height of its power. In a dark, smoky room, a Chinese alchemist is doing an experiment in his search for the secret of eternal life. He heats sulphur and charcoal together, which he has done before. But then he adds a material called saltpetre (potassium nitrate) to the mixture. There is a flash, and a loud bang. The alchemist runs from the room, yelling, as the house begins to burn. He has discovered gunpowder.

When gunpowder was first made, no one could understand how it worked. They did not know that burning and explosions are chemical reactions. Alchemists, who were the chemists of that time, thought that fire was an **element**. **Combustion** (burning) is probably the most important of all chemical reactions. We use fires to keep warm and cook food. Most of our electricity is made in power stations that burn fuel. The engines in vehicles also burn fuel. Even our bodies get energy from food through a very slow type of combustion.

Other reactions

Combustion is not the only chemical reaction we rely on. Hundreds of other chemical reactions are essential to our lives. Most manufacturing and building materials are made using processes that involve chemical reactions.

WHAT IS AN ALCHEMIST?

Early chemists were called alchemists. Alchemists carried out many chemical reactions, but their main aims were to discover the secret of eternal life, and to find a way of turning other metals into gold. Alchemists existed in China as early as 800 BC. Until the development of chemistry in the 18th century, many people who were interested in chemical reactions studied alchemy.

Chemical reactions separate metals from their **ores** (the rocks they are found in) and produce plastics from petroleum (oil). The paint on your bedroom wall, the dye in your clothes, the medicines in the first-aid box, soap, and other cleaning materials – all these are made using chemical reactions.

Since the discovery of gunpowder, chemists have learned a huge amount about chemical reactions. A chain of important discoveries has inspired scientists, and enabled them to progress from gunpowder to laser chemistry. This book follows that chain. It explains how explosives were made from manure. It describes how one man explained combustion and founded chemistry as a science. It tells the story of the woman who looked into the heart of **atoms**. And it describes how modern chemists can use computers to find out about the reactions of substances that have not yet been made by scientists.

The first stage in getting metal from an ore is often smelting (heating the ore until it becomes molten). These workers in Guatemala are smelting gold and silver.

Discovering gunpowder

When Chinese alchemists first made gunpowder, they used it to treat skin diseases and to produce smoke to get rid of insects. Soon gunpowder was being used to make fireworks. It was not long before military commanders realized that this exploding powder could also be used to make weapons.

Berthold Schwarz was a 14th-century German monk and alchemist. He was one of the first Europeans to experiment with gunpowder. In this picture he is setting off a charge of gunpowder, which fires a metal block into the air.

The earliest gunpowder weapons were "paper bombs". These were balls of papier mâché, filled with powder, and fired at the enemy with a catapult. Later, metal balls were used. These were better weapons because they sent sharp pieces of metal flying everywhere when they exploded. The Chinese also developed "arrows of flaming fire" (rocket-powered arrows) and tubes filled with gunpowder that were used as flame-throwers.

Ehrwürdigen vnd Sinnreiche Patters Bertold Schwartz genandt, Franciscaner Ordens, Doctor, Alchimist vnd Erfinder der freyen kunst des Buchsenschiessens, im Jar 1320.

Sehet da was thüet die zeit, vnd die Natur darneben durch Scharffsinnigeleücht, offt mals an den Tag geben Des Buchsenschiessens kunst, Erzeügt durch Fewres art vnd aus der Natur dünst, zu mal geboren wardt.

Gunpowder goes west

The secret of how to make gunpowder did not stay in China for long. By the 13th century, Arab alchemists knew how it was made. European alchemists then learned the secret from them. Soon gunpowder was being made in Europe. From the 1350s until about 1620, two of the main ingredients for making gunpowder were urine and manure. These substances were scraped off the walls of stables. They were then mixed together with wood ash in large heaps, which were left to ripen like compost. After several months, a white powder began to appear on the heaps. This powder was collected and purified to make saltpetre.

Early cannons were called bombards. They were made like iron barrels, with rings of iron holding together a cylinder made of several iron bars.

At first, soldiers using gunpowder had to mix the powdered ingredients (charcoal, sulphur, and saltpetre) in the right amounts. However, in the early 15th century gunpowder makers began to mix the ingredients together in water, then dry the mixture out to produce ready-mixed gunpowder.

Initially, gunpowder was used in cannons that could batter down the thickest walls. Later, it was also used in guns. By the end of the 14th century, gunpowder had changed the way that armies fought wars. As gunpowder became important in warfare, chemists who could produce good-quality gunpowder also became important.

Gunpowder was mainly used for fireworks and weapons. However, there is a story that in the 16th century a minor Chinese official called Wan Hu built a rocket-powered flying chair. The chair had 47 rockets attached to the back, and 2 kites to lift it into the air. Wan Hu made the first test flight. When the rockets were lit, there was a huge explosion and a cloud of white smoke. When the smoke cleared, there was no sign of Wan Hu or his chair, and he was never seen again.

Burning and breathing

By the 17th century, many countries had factories that could produce good-quality gunpowder. However, no one could explain what happened when gunpowder exploded.

Gunpowder explodes by burning very fast and producing gases. In the early 17th century, no one understood that air and other gases could take part in chemical reactions. But then three English scholars took the first steps towards understanding **combustion** and gases.

This fireball was produced by gunpowder exploding. Gunpowder burns very rapidly, generating large amounts of gas and heat.

More than an alchemist

Robert Boyle (1627–1691) was an alchemist, but he was also a natural philosopher. This was the name that scientists gave themselves in the 17th century. Natural philosophers believed in the importance of doing experiments to find things out. In 1659, Boyle began a series of investigations with a new machine that had recently been invented – the **vacuum** pump. Boyle and his assistant, Robert Hooke (1635–1703), used the pump to remove the air from a glass jar containing a red-hot metal plate.

If Boyle dropped some paper on the plate, nothing happened. But as soon as air was let into the jar, the paper caught fire. He also did experiments with a mouse in the jar. He found that when the air was removed the mouse could not breathe.

From these experiments, Boyle reasoned that air was needed for combustion and for animals to stay alive. These ideas seem very obvious now, but at the time no one had thought about air in this way.

Not all the air

Another Englishman, a doctor called John Mayow (1640–1679), took Boyle and Hooke's experiments further. John Mayow burned a candle inside a jar that was cut off from the surrounding air by water. As the candle burned, some of the air was used up in the chemical reaction of burning. When about one-fifth of the air was gone, the candle went out. This experiment showed that only a part of the air is involved in combustion.

This is an original illustration showing one of John Mayow's experiments. Mayow used a magnifying glass to light the candle inside the jar. As the candle burned the air, the water level in the jar rose.

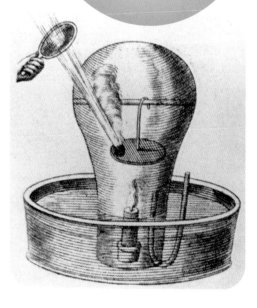

Mayow came very close to discovering the vital ingredient in air that caused combustion. But before anyone could take his ideas further, chemistry went off down a blind alley, looking for a mysterious substance called **phlogiston**.

Chemists of the air

The ancient Greeks and most alchemists believed that fire was a substance, like earth, air, and water. By Robert Boyle's time, in the 17th century, most people realized that fire was not a substance but was actually a type of chemical reaction.

When a fuel burns, it produces flames and smoke. A German doctor called Georg Stahl suggested that when something burns, it gives off a substance called phlogiston. Many scientists were impressed with Stahl's ideas. For over 70 years, they tried to find evidence of phlogiston.

Different "airs"

According to Stahl, when something burns it releases phlogiston into the air. Many scientists therefore began to investigate air. At that time, any gas was thought of as a type of "air". Investigators looked at many different reactions that produce gases, and soon they were finding many types of "air". A Scottish doctor, Joseph Black, discovered a gas that he called "fixed air". Nothing could burn in this "air", and it turned lime water milky. Today, we call it carbon dioxide. An English scientist, Joseph Priestley (1733–1804), discovered another gas, which he called "dephlogisticated air". Materials burned much better in this gas than in ordinary air. This gas would later be renamed oxygen.

This drawing shows equipment Joseph Priestley used to investigate different "airs" (gases). Priestley discovered 10 gases, including oxygen, hydrogen chloride, nitrous oxide and sulphur dioxide.

In 1766 another English scientist, Henry Cavendish (1731–1810), found a new type of "air" when he was experimenting with mixtures of **acids** and metals. This new gas was **inflammable**: it burned with a "pop" when he put a flame to it. It was also lighter than air, or any other gas. When Cavendish mixed this gas with Priestley's dephlogisticated air (oxygen) and added a spark, he produced water. He decided that this inflammable gas must be phlogiston. Today we know it as hydrogen.

JACQUES CHARLES'S STORY

This illustration shows Jacques Charles's first hydrogen balloon flight in 1783. He called his balloon *La Charlière*.

Jacques Charles (1746–1823) was a French scientist and daredevil. When Charles learned that Henry Cavendish's inflammable air was four times lighter than normal air, he had the idea of using it to make a balloon. In December 1783, only weeks after the Montgolfier Brothers made the first ever balloon flight, Charles flew to a height of 3 kilometres (nearly 2 miles) in the first hydrogen balloon flight. Charles also used hydrogen to do some fire-breathing. He inhaled some hydrogen, then set light to it as he breathed out. However, when he tried the same thing with a mixture of hydrogen and air, the mixture exploded, and he nearly blew his teeth out.

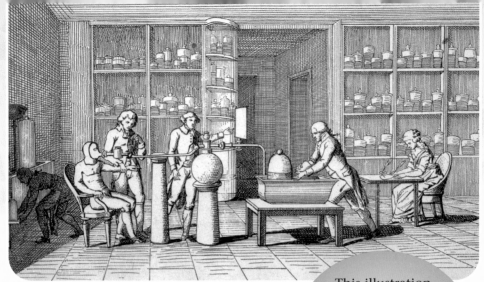

Explaining combustion

Stahl's phlogiston theory appeared to make sense, but in fact it was completely wrong. Towards the last years of the 18th century, a French scientist, Antoine Lavoisier (1743–1794), found the key to combustion by turning phlogiston theory on its head.

This illustration shows an experiment with breathing in Lavoisier's laboratory. Lavoisier's wife Marie Anne (right) worked as his assistant. She helped with experiments, wrote up notes, and drew diagrams.

Lavoisier was a very painstaking scientist, who weighed and measured everything accurately, and carefully recorded his results. He had tremendous energy, and carried out hundreds of different experiments. In addition, Lavoisier had the vision to link together the results of his experiments, and come up with important and original conclusions.

Lavoisier did many experiments to try and work out what happened during combustion. Some of his experiments were similar to those of earlier scientists. Like John Mayow, he found that part of the air was used up when something burned. He also found, like Joseph Priestley, that he could produce a gas that was much better than normal air for burning things. He renamed this gas oxygen. And he suggested that it was involved in the chemical reaction that happened when something burned. The burning substance reacts with oxygen from the air to produce carbon dioxide and other gases, as well as a lot of heat and flames. This type of reaction, in which oxygen combines with another substance, is called **oxidation**.

Lavoisier's death

Lavoisier published a book containing all his ideas about combustion and chemistry in 1789. In the same year, the French Revolution began. The ordinary people of France had been suffering great hardship because of poor harvests and rising taxes, while the king and the aristocrats enjoyed enormous wealth. The people's resentment eventually led to a violent uprising, in which many nobles and others seen as "enemies of the people" were executed. Although Lavoisier was a chemist, he also worked as a tax collector to earn money. Because of his tax collecting, Lavoisier was arrested and imprisoned by the Revolutionary Council. A powerful friend pleaded for Lavoisier's life, but the plea was unsuccessful, and he was executed in 1794.

TALKING SCIENCE

"It took them only an instant to cut off that head, but France may not produce another like it in a century."
The mathematician Joseph-Louis Lagrange, on Lavoisier's death

Lavoisier was executed using a guillotine like the ones shown here.

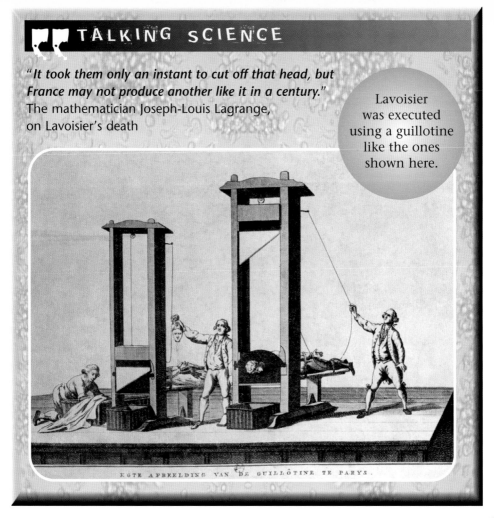

EGTE AFBEELDING VAN DE GUILLÔTINE TE PARYS.

Weighing atoms

Lavoisier's ideas were not immediately accepted. Many older scientists were unwilling to give up the old **phlogiston** theory. However, some of the younger scientists soon took to Lavoisier's ideas and methods. Chemists began to use careful measurements in all the experiments they carried out.

Once chemists started measuring, they found that substances combined in predictable ways. Chemists already knew that **acids** and **bases** were chemical opposites. But then a German chemist, Jeremias Richter (1762–1807), measured how much acid he had to mix with a base to get a neutral mixture. He found that a fixed amount of a particular acid would neutralize a particular base. This amount was the same every time.

Baking soda is an alkali, while vinegar is an acid. If you mix the two together, gas produced in the neutralization reaction makes large amounts of froth.

? WHAT IS NEUTRALIZATION?

Acids and **alkalis** (sometimes known as bases) are chemical opposites. They are at opposite ends of the pH scale. Strong acids have a pH around 1, while strong alkalis have a pH around 14. A liquid that is in the middle, with a pH of about 7, is said to be neutral. Water is a neutral liquid. When an acid and an alkali are mixed in the right amounts, they form a neutral liquid (pH 7). Neutralization is a chemical reaction. The acid and alkali react to form a salt and water.

A French chemist, Joseph Proust (1754–1826), found that other substances also mixed in fixed amounts. He found, for instance, that table salt (sodium chloride) always contained 1.5 times as much chlorine as sodium. This is because chlorine **atoms** weigh 1.5 times more than sodium atoms.

John Dalton made discoveries in other fields besides chemistry. He was the first person to describe colour blindness. He was also one of the first people to take accurate daily weather records.

Proust and Richter almost certainly knew about each other's discoveries. Unlike alchemists, who kept their methods secret, chemists liked to share the details of their work with each other. Chemists and other scientists published their work in journals or letters. Sharing information meant that scientific knowledge progressed much more quickly.

Multiple mixtures

In England, a chemist called John Dalton (1766–1844) found that he could combine some substances in more than one way. For instance, if he mixed carbon with a certain amount of oxygen, he got one type of gas. However, if he mixed carbon with twice as much oxygen, he could produce a different gas.

Dalton explained his results by proposing that substances were made up of very tiny particles. He called these particles atoms. In the first gas Dalton made, each atom of carbon joined with one of oxygen to form carbon monoxide. However, when he added twice as much oxygen, each carbon atom joined with two oxygen atoms to form a different gas – carbon dioxide.

Different sizes

Other scientists before Dalton had suggested that substances were made up of tiny particles. But Dalton proposed something new. He suggested that each **element** (a material such as carbon or oxygen, which cannot be broken down into simpler substances) had atoms of a different size and weight. Most importantly, he worked out a way of weighing these atoms – or at least of working out how much heavier the atoms of one element were than those of another. First, he assumed that when substances combined in the simplest way, they combined in a 1 to 1 ratio. He therefore assumed that the simplest combination of carbon and oxygen, with three parts carbon and four parts oxygen, was carbon monoxide. If this was correct, then a carbon atom must be three-quarters the weight of an oxygen atom.

This is John Dalton's original table of elements, compiled in 1803. The atoms of different elements were represented by symbols, and their relative atomic weights, compared to hydrogen, were listed.

ELEMENTS

		w.t				w.t
⊙	Hydrogen.	1	⊕	Strontian		46
◐	Azote	5	✳	Barytes		68
●	Carbon	5	Ⓘ	Iron		50
○	Oxygen	7	Ⓩ	Zinc		56
☮	Phosphorus	9	Ⓒ	Copper		56
⊕	Sulphur	13	Ⓛ	Lead		90
◉	Magnesia	20	Ⓢ	Silver		190
⊝	Lime	24	ⓓ	Gold		190
◑	Soda	28	Ⓟ	Platina		190
⦀	Potash	42	✺	Mercury		167

Atomic weights

After studying many combinations of elements and measuring the weights that combined together, Dalton came up with a list of **atomic weights**. These were not actual weights. Dalton compared the weight of each atom to that of hydrogen, which he gave the atomic weight of 1. Carbon, for instance, he found to be 5 times heavier than hydrogen, so he gave it an atomic weight of 5.

Dalton's atomic weight idea was tremendously important for chemistry. Unfortunately, he got most of his weights wrong! Carbon, for instance, has an atomic weight of 12, not 5.

This table shows some of Dalton's atomic weights for different elements, compared with the modern atomic weights. In many cases, Dalton's atomic weights were about half the correct values.

Element	Dalton's atomic weights	Modern atomic weights
Hydrogen	1	1
Azote (nitrogen)	5	14
Carbon	5	12
Oxygen	7	16
Phosphorous	9	31
Sulphur	13	28
Magnesia (magnesium)	20	24
Strontian (strontium)	46	87
Iron	50	56
Zinc	56	65
Copper	56	64
Lead	90	207
Silver	190	107
Gold	190	197

Dalton assumed, incorrectly, that when substances combined in the simplest way, they always combined in a 1 to 1 ratio. For instance, he assumed that water was one oxygen atom combined with one hydrogen atom. But, as we now know, water has two hydrogens and one oxygen (H_2O).

WHAT WAS DALTON'S ATOMIC THEORY?

In working out his atomic weights, Dalton made the following assumptions about the nature of atoms and elements.

1) All matter is made of atoms.
2) Atoms cannot be divided or destroyed.
3) All atoms of a given element are identical and weigh the same.
4) **Compounds** are formed by a combination of two or more different types of atom.
5) A chemical reaction is a rearrangement of atoms.

This was the first attempt to describe chemistry in terms of atoms. Dalton's assumptions proved to be broadly correct, although we now know for instance that assumption 2 is wrong (atoms can be divided). Nevertheless, for the first time, chemists had an idea of what was going on in a chemical reaction – atoms were being rearranged.

How elements combine

Some chemists quickly saw the importance of Dalton's **atoms** and **atomic weights**. One of these was Jöns Berzelius (1779–1848). Berzelius was a brilliant Swedish experimenter and teacher. When he read about Dalton's work, he agreed with his theories but not with his experimental results. He began to revise Dalton's atomic weights.

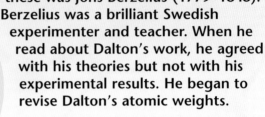

This drawing, dated around 1810, shows Jöns Berzelius, the Swedish chemist who found out the correct atomic weights of many substances. He also discovered three elements: selenium, thorium, and cerium.

Berzelius did most of his research in a laboratory at his house. He carried out hundreds of experiments in which he worked out what weights of two **elements** combined together. From these experiments, he was able to work out accurate atomic weights for the 43 or so elements that were known at the time, as well as many combinations of elements known as **compounds**.

Berzelius's atomic weights for most elements are close to modern values. For instance, he realized that in water two hydrogen atoms combine with one oxygen atom. This meant that he got the atomic weights of both hydrogen and oxygen right.

TALKING SCIENCE

"The laboratory consisted of two ordinary rooms furnished in the simplest possible way; there were no furnaces or draught places... In the other room were the balances, and some cupboards containing instruments. In the neighbouring kitchen, in which Anna prepared the meals, was a furnace and the never-cool sand-bath."
Friedrich Wöhler's first impressions of Berzelius's home laboratory

Writing down reactions

Berzelius wanted a simple way to write down how much of each element there was in a chemical compound. In 1811, he came up with a system that we still use today. He gave each element a one- or two-letter abbreviation, such as H for hydrogen and O for oxygen. He then used numbers to show how many atoms of each element were in a compound. For instance, water (which has two hydrogens joined to one oxygen) is written H_2O. This is known as a chemical formula.

Chemists very quickly began to use Berzelius's chemical notation. Once they could write chemical formulas, they soon began to write out chemical reactions. Written reactions are called chemical equations. For instance, the chemical equation for making water from hydrogen and oxygen gases is written as:

$$2H_2 \quad + \quad O_2 \quad = \quad 2H_2O$$
hydrogen gas   oxygen gas   water

The equation has two **molecules** of hydrogen gas and two of water, because otherwise it would not balance: there would be one fewer oxygen atoms at the end of the reaction than at the start.

This picture shows Lavoisier proving that water is a compound of hydrogen and oxygen. The grey cylinders hold the oxygen and hydrogen, which are piped into the flask in the centre. A spark causes the hydrogen to burn in the oxygen, producing water.

Electric reactions

This is Volta's original battery, invented in 1799. It was made from alternating discs of copper and zinc, separated by pads of cloth that had been soaked in salty water.

Atomic theory was one of many breakthroughs in chemistry in the early 19th century. Another important discovery was the connection between electricity and chemical reactions. At this time, electricity was a new discovery. There were batteries, but no generators, lights, or other machines powered by electricity.

In 1800, the Italian scientist Alessandro Volta (1745–1827) announced the invention of the first battery, called a voltaic pile. This battery was made of a pile of metal discs separated by pads of wet cloth. Before this, electricity could only be produced in bursts, by storing static electricity. Volta's pile gave a constant electric current. Berzelius read about Volta's battery and immediately built one of his own. He used it to see if treatment with electricity helped patients with various illnesses. The treatment did not help the patients, but Berzelius did not lose interest in investigating electricity.

HOW DID VOLTA FIND OUT HOW TO GENERATE CONTINUOUS ELECTRICITY?

In the 1770s, the Italian anatomist Luigi Galvani (1737–1798) started using electrostatic machines to stimulate animal muscles. During these experiments, Galvani found that he could make the muscles work without adding electricity, if he hung the muscle tissues on an iron rail using a copper hook. Galvani thought that muscles contained a force (which he called "animal electricity") that made the muscles work. However, Volta realized that the muscle's movement simply indicated that electricity was flowing. The electricity actually came from the contact of the two wet metals (iron and copper). After many experiments he found that copper and zinc discs, separated by cardboard soaked in salty water, could produce a continuous electric current.

WHAT SPEEDS UP CHEMICAL REACTIONS?

Berzelius made another important discovery. He found that some substances can speed up a chemical reaction without themselves being used up. Berzelius called these substances **catalysts**. Platinum, for instance, is a catalyst that can speed up reactions between gases. Today, platinum is used in car exhausts to help absorb polluting gases from the exhaust and stop them being released into the atmosphere. In living things, protein catalysts, known as **enzymes**, play a vital part in controlling the working of living cells.

Separating chemicals

Berzelius became interested in using his battery to split up chemical **compounds**. He showed that the electricity could be used to split water into two gases – hydrogen and oxygen. He also found that other substances could be split this way. This process of using electricity to split chemicals became known as **electrolysis**. But while Berzelius was splitting substances in Sweden, another scientist, working in London, was building giant batteries to do experiments of his own.

This is the modern apparatus used for the electrolysis of water. The black hook shapes in the beaker are electrodes. The positive electrode (left) produces bubbles of oxygen, while the negative electrode (right) produces bubbles of hydrogen.

The laughing chemist

Berzelius valued accuracy and did not publish results until he was sure they were right. Humphry Davy (1778–1829) was a very different sort of person. One of his first experiments was to test the effects of various gases to see if they were medically useful. He nearly killed himself in one of these experiments, by breathing in carbon monoxide and hydrogen. However, he found that one gas, nitrous oxide, made him feel wonderfully happy. He also found that it was a good anaesthetic (it dulled pain). Nitrous oxide quickly became popular as a way of having fun, but at the time it was not used as an anaesthetic.

In this cartoon of a lecture at the Royal Institution, a volunteer is being given nitrous oxide as a "laughing gas". The lecturer is Thomas Garrett, while Humphry Davy holds the bellows in the background.

Sparks fly

Davy became a lecturer in chemistry at the Royal Institution in London. The Royal Institution had a large battery, and Davy soon began using it to carry out chemical experiments. He quickly found ways to improve the battery, and built a more powerful one. Like Berzelius, he realized that the battery could be used to split chemical compounds. In 1807, he tried his battery on two substances, potash and common salt. The results were two new **elements** – potassium and sodium – discovered in the space of a week.

⚡ TALKING SCIENCE

"When he saw the globules of potassium burst through the crust of potash, and take fire... he could not contain his joy – he actually danced about the room in ecstatic delight; some little time was required for him to compose himself to continue the experiment."

Edmund Davy (Humphry's cousin), describing Davy's joy on discovering potassium

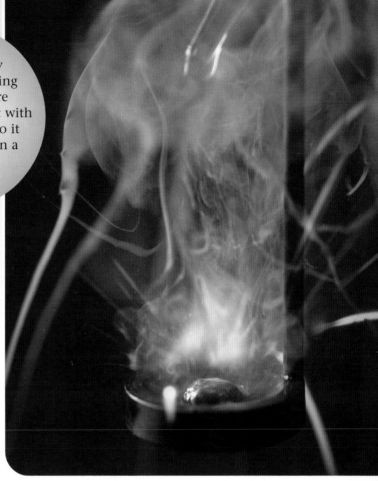

Potassium reacts violently with water, bursting into flames. Pure potassium can react with water in the air, so it has to be stored in a liquid such as paraffin.

Davy demonstrated his discoveries in his lectures at the Royal Institution. He was a great showman. He used his batteries to produce dramatic sparks, and dropped pieces of potassium into water, where they "skimmed about excitedly … and soon burned with a lovely lavender light". In 1808, Davy discovered another element, boron. He also showed that a chemical then called "oxymuriatic acid" did not contain any oxygen and was in fact an element, which he called chlorine.

Electrochemical theory

In Sweden, Berzelius also continued to do important electrochemical research. He suggested that all chemical compounds could be split into a negative or acidic part, which is attracted to the positive **electrode** of a battery, and a basic or **alkaline** part, which is attracted to the negative electrode. This theory worked quite well for many materials.

Electric chemistry gets rules

Humphry Davy's exciting lectures inspired many people to take up science. One of these people was a young bookbinder's assistant called Michael Faraday (1791–1867). Faraday decided he wanted to make science his career. He made a book of notes of Davy's lecture, and sent it to Davy, asking him for a job.

At first, Davy had no work for Faraday. Then, in 1812, Davy injured his eyes in an experiment that went wrong. He remembered the young man who had written to him, and decided to give Faraday a job. Faraday worked with Davy for almost eight years. During this time he learned a great deal and developed his skills as a chemist.

This illustration shows Faraday lecturing at the Royal Institution, in London, in 1855. Prince Albert (Queen Victoria's husband) and two of his sons are sitting in the front row, facing Faraday.

Electrical interests

In 1819, Hans Oersted (1777–1851), a Danish scientist, discovered that when electricity ran through a wire it produced a magnetic field. An English scientist, called William Wollaston, suggested that the magnetic field would form a circle around the wire. He predicted that two electric wires could be made to circle each other. He and Davy carried out the experiment, but could not make it work.

WHAT ARE THE CHRISTMAS LECTURES?

Faraday used to give children's lectures every Christmas. These lectures are still given every Christmas at the Royal Institution, in London, and are also shown on television. In 1860 Faraday published a book, *The Chemical History of a Candle*, based on his lectures. The book explained **combustion** and many other chemical topics. It is still in print.

Faraday heard about Wollaston and Davy's experiment. Over the summer of 1821, he tried it out himself. He was able to make a magnet rotate around an electric wire, and an electric wire rotate around a magnet. He wrote up his experiment, but did not credit Wollaston. Several of Wollaston's friends wrote to Faraday to protest about this. Faraday apologized, and in later writings acknowledged Wollaston's contribution. However, Davy did not forgive Faraday for his mistake for many years.

Laws of electrochemistry

In 1833, Faraday developed a new theory about what happens when electricity is passed through a **solution**. He suggested that when electricity causes a substance to decompose, the electricity splits the compound into two fragments, one positively charged and one negatively charged. Faraday called these charged fragments **ions**. This term is still used today for charged **atoms** or **molecules**. Faraday also discovered that the amount of a substance that is deposited at an electrode or dissolved from an electrode is proportional to the amount of electricity passed through the electrical cell. Faraday's discoveries gave scientists a much greater understanding of how electricity and chemistry are related.

The chemistry of carbon

By the 1820s, some chemists were beginning to understand much more about chemical reactions. But there was one group of **compounds** that was still little understood. These were compounds made from carbon – organic compounds.

The Swedish scientist Berzelius called carbon compounds "organic chemicals" because most of them came from living things. Chemists could extract all types of compounds from plants and animals. They could also make products such as soap, dyes, and perfumes. However, they could not make any organic chemicals directly. This all changed with the work of a German chemist called Friedrich Wöhler (1800–1882).

Making organic chemicals

Wöhler was a pupil and later a friend of Berzelius. In 1828, while working in Berlin, in Germany, he made an astonishing discovery. He reacted silver cyanate with ammonium chloride, expecting to get a compound called ammonium cyanate. In fact he got a white solid that proved to be urea, a substance found in urine.

This was the first time that an organic compound had been made artificially. Some scientists had thought it was impossible to make organic compounds because they contained a "vital substance" that was only found in living things.

WHAT IS AN ORGANIC COMPOUND?

Living things consist of complex chemicals that are made mostly from carbon and hydrogen. They may also contain other **elements** such as oxygen and nitrogen. Nearly all carbon compounds are classed as organic compounds, but there are a few exceptions. Graphite and diamond, which are pure carbon, do not count as organic compounds. Other, non-carbon compounds are known as inorganic compounds.

"I can no longer, so to speak, hold my chemical water and must tell you that I can make urea without needing a kidney, whether of man or dog; the ammonium salt of cyanic acid is urea."
Friedrich Wöhler, in a letter to Berzelius

Once Wöhler's success became known, other chemists also found ways to make organic compounds. In 1845, a pupil of Wöhler's called Adolf Kolbe made acetic acid, the main ingredient of vinegar. And in the 1850s, the French chemist Marcellin Berthelot (1827–1907) made many organic compounds. Later, Berthelot went a step further and began to make organic compounds that were not found in nature.

Some dyes are natural (rather than man-made) organic compounds. Indigo, a natural blue dye made from a tropical plant, has been used for centuries. This Nigerian villager is soaking some clothing in indigo dye.

Combining power

Although chemists were now able to classify different organic compounds within groups or types, they still did not know how the **atoms** in organic compounds were actually organized.

The first clue as to how organic compounds were structured came from the English chemist Edward Frankland (1825–1899). While he was studying organic compounds containing metals, he noticed that different metals always combined with the same number of other atoms or groups. For instance, silver always combined with one organic group, while zinc could combine with two.

Frankland suggested that all elements have a particular combining power. In other words, they can connect to a particular number of other **elements** or groups. This combining power is now known as **valency**.

The chemist Friedrich Kekulé originally trained as an architect. This may have helped him to visualize the structures of several organic compounds.

Atom	Symbol	Valency	Hydrogen compound
Lithium	Li	1	LiH
Beryllium	Be	2	BeH_2
Boron	B	3	BH_3
Carbon	C	4	CH_4
Nitrogen	N	3	NH_3
Oxygen	O	2	H_2O

Valency can be simply defined as the number of hydrogen (H) atoms an element can combine with. These are some examples of valencies.

Carbon chains

Friedrich Kekulé (1829–1896), a German chemist, took Frankland's idea of valency and applied it to organic compounds. He discovered that carbon has a valency of 4. He also saw that the structure of many organic compounds could be explained by carbon atoms joining together in chains. Each carbon atom in a chain is joined to two others. The other "spaces" on each carbon atom are usually filled by hydrogen atoms, but other atoms or functional groups can also be attached.

Using the idea of four-handed carbon atoms that could form chains, scientists could write down structures for many organic compounds. However, a few compounds did not seem to fit Kekulé's theory. One of these was benzene, which has the formula C_6H_6. Kekulé could not work out how to explain this formula. Eventually, after seven years of puzzling, Kekulé found the answer in 1865. He proposed that benzene was a ring of carbons, rather than a chain. The ring structure was an important discovery, because many important biological compounds, such as sugars, are rings of carbon atoms.

These diagrams show the structure of hexane, and the structure that Kekulé suggested for benzene. The green circles are carbon atoms, and the yellow circles are hydrogen.

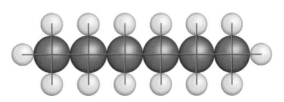

hexane (C_6H_{14})

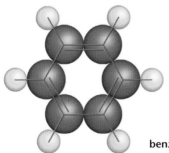

benzene (C_6H_6)

Explaining heat

Most chemical reactions need energy to get started. This energy is usually heat. For example, a fire will burn for a long time if it has fuel, but it needs the heat from a match to get it going. The French chemist Lavoisier thought that heat was an **element**. But studies by physicists in the early 1800s showed that it was a form of energy. Soon chemists began looking at the heat and energy changes in chemical reactions.

The study of changes in heat (or other energy) during a process is known as **thermodynamics**. By studying the thermodynamics of chemical reactions, chemists hoped to be able to tell whether or not a reaction was likely to happen spontaneously (naturally).

The American Count Rumford, born Benjamin Thompson (1753–1814), was one of the first people to suggest that heat was energy, rather than a substance. He got his ideas from watching cannons being bored (drilled out). This process generated a lot of heat through friction.

Changes in heat

In the 1840s, the Swiss chemist Germain Hess (1802–1850) showed that the heat produced (or absorbed) during a chemical reaction was the same, no matter how the reaction occurred.

Then, in the 1860s the French chemist Marcellin Berthelot (1827–1907) began to study the heat changes in chemical reactions. He built a piece of apparatus called a bomb calorimeter, in which chemical reactions took place in a container surrounded by a water bath. Any heat given out or taken in during the reaction affected the temperature of the water in the water bath. This change could be measured.

Using the bomb calorimeter, Berthelot and other chemists were able to measure the heat changes in a wide range of chemical reactions. They found that most reactions were **exothermic** (gave out heat), and Berthelot concluded that all spontaneous chemical reactions were exothermic. However, some reactions were found to be **endothermic** – they took in heat.

WHAT ARE EXOTHERMIC AND ENDOTHERMIC REACTIONS?

Most spontaneous chemical reactions (ones that keep going by themselves) are exothermic. This means that the reaction produces heat. Any kind of **combustion** is obviously exothermic, but so are many other reactions. For instance, the mortar used in the past for cementing bricks together contained quicklime (calcium oxide). When water was added to the lime, it got very hot as it reacted with the water to form calcium hydroxide. A similar reaction happens as concrete sets.

A few chemical reactions are endothermic – they take in heat from their surroundings. For example, if ammonium nitrate crystals are dissolved in water, the container the solution is in becomes cold. This is because the reaction between ammonium nitrate and water takes heat from its surroundings.

Big business

In the early 1800s, there were few jobs for chemists, but by the 1850s things were changing. Chemistry had become a popular subject, and many people studied it. Towards the end of the 19th century, advances in both organic and inorganic chemistry meant that chemical reactions became big business.

One of the first big successes for organic chemistry came in 1856, when an 18-year-old London chemistry student called William Perkin (1838–1907) tried to make a drug from coal. Perkin's teacher, August von Hoffmann, suggested that if Perkin wanted a challenge he could perhaps try making quinine from coal tar (a thick, sticky liquid extracted from coal). At the time, quinine was the only effective treatment for malaria.

This is William Perkin at the age of 14. He discovered the dye mauveine just 4 years after this photo was taken.

A lucky accident

During the Easter holidays, Perkin decided to try making quinine at home. His first attempt produced some black gunk in the bottom of the reaction flask. When he tried to clean out the flask with alcohol, he got a brilliant purple liquid. Dissolving the "gunk" in alcohol had created an excellent dye.

The purple colour that Perkin had made became known as mauveine, or mauve. It was the first **synthetic** dye. Purple dyes were popular at the time, but the natural ones were not very good.

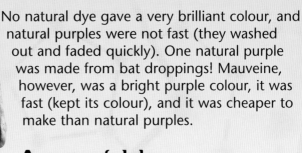

No natural dye gave a very brilliant colour, and natural purples were not fast (they washed out and faded quickly). One natural purple was made from bat droppings! Mauveine, however, was a bright purple colour, it was fast (kept its colour), and it was cheaper to make than natural purples.

A successful dye

With his father's help, Perkin set up a factory to make mauveine. Soon after production began, Queen Victoria wore a dress dyed with mauveine, and the colour became very fashionable.

In the late 1860s, the colour mauve became less fashionable. But by this time Perkin had made several other synthetic dyes. However, by the 1870s Germany had taken the lead in the dye market (see page 34). In 1874 Perkin, who was by this time a millionaire, sold his dye factory to a German firm.

This is William Perkin's original stoppered bottle of mauveine dye, labelled "Original Mauveine prepared by Sir William Perkin in 1856" (probably repackaged in 1906).

THAT'S AMAZING!

Many synthetic dyes have been made since Perkin first made mauve. The biggest group are known as azo dyes. The first azo dye was made in 1862. When the first synthetic fibres were made (see page 49), new dyes were produced that could dye synthetic fabrics. In 1956, fibre-reactive dyes were developed. These can combine chemically with the material being dyed and so cannot be washed out.

German chemicals

Several chemists, particularly in Germany, soon found other chemicals that made excellent dyes. In 1869 two German chemists, Carl Graebe and Carl Liebermann, made a red dye called alizarin. William Perkin also made alizarin at about the same time. Alizarin is the pigment that gives the vegetable dye called madder its red colour. Madder was made from the ground-up roots of the madder plant. The synthetic version of the dye proved to be much cheaper to make than natural madder.

Graebe and Liebermann worked for the German company BASF. Among other things, BASF made dyes from natural materials. One of the most important dyes they made was indigo, a blue colour. From 1865 onwards, the German chemist Johann von Baeyer (1835–1917) tried to **synthesize** indigo from simple chemicals. Baeyer worked on making indigo for many years and finally succeeded in 1880. However, it was another 17 years before indigo could be mass-produced. This was because it took a long time to find reasonably priced, easily available chemicals, from which large quantities of dye could be produced.

Germany remains an important centre for dyeing even today.

In the 20th century, when electricity became much cheaper, some chemicals were made using **electrolysis**. This factory is making sodium hydroxide by electrolysis of brine (salt dissolved in water).

Industrial chemicals

In the late 19th century, other chemicals besides dyes were in great demand. One of the earliest industrial chemicals (chemicals made on a large scale in factories) was soda ash (sodium carbonate). This is used to make soap and glass. In 1790, the French chemist Nicolas Leblanc (1742–1806) developed a process for making soda ash from sodium chloride (table salt) and sulphuric acid.

The Leblanc process was used to make soda ash for nearly 100 years. However, in the 1860s it was replaced by the Solvay process, in which sodium chloride was treated with ammonia and carbon dioxide. The Solvay process replaced the Leblanc process because it could be used to produce soda ash more cheaply.

WHAT IS SODA ASH USED FOR?

Soda ash is used for making glass and soap. To make glass, a special type of sand is heated until it melts, then cooled slowly. However, the sand melts at a very high temperature. Adding soda ash to the mixture makes the sand melt at a lower temperature, which saves a lot of time and energy.

Soda ash is also used in soap-making. Soap is made by mixing fats or oils with a hot **alkali** such as sodium hydroxide. Sodium carbonate is added to the soap to give it better washing ability.

Keeping the temperature down

Other industrially made chemicals included sulphuric acid, ammonia, and nitric acid. They were used in the manufacture of fertilizers, dyes, drugs, explosives, detergents, and for many other purposes.

The processes for making these chemicals used **catalysts**. For instance, iron was used as a catalyst when making ammonia, and vanadium pentoxide was used for making sulphuric acid. Without catalysts, the reactions did not happen quickly enough, or had to be done at extremely high temperatures and pressures.

One of the most important of these methods was the Haber process for making ammonia (NH_3). It was developed by Fritz Haber between 1904 and 1909. Ammonia is an essential ingredient for making fertilizers and explosives (see opposite). During the 19th century, it was made from natural deposits of nitrate that came from Chile.

Modern industrial plants can manufacture chemicals in very large quantities. This particular plant produces a range of chemicals from crude petroleum (oil).

The Haber process makes ammonia directly from its **elements**, hydrogen and nitrogen. These two gases are combined at high temperature and pressure, using iron as a catalyst for the reaction.

Replacing gunpowder

Another chemical that was needed in large quantities was gunpowder. In the 1890s, the traditional "black powder" was replaced by a better, smokeless powder that used the explosive nitrocellulose (see below).

THAT'S AMAZING!

In 1845, the German chemist Christian Schönbein (1799–1868) spilled nitric acid and sulphuric acid on his kitchen table. He mopped up the spill with the nearest thing he could find – his wife's cotton apron. He hung the apron near the stove to dry, and – BANG! – the apron exploded. Schönbein had found a way to make nitrocellulose, or guncotton. At first nitrocellulose was too unstable to use safely. However, in 1889 two English chemists, Sir James Dewar and Frederick Abel, developed a stable form of nitrocellulose, called cordite, that could be used in weapons.

Another high explosive developed in the mid-1800s was nitroglycerine. This liquid explosive was very sensitive to shock. Nitroglycerine was so dangerous to make and use that for many years few people attempted to produce it.

The Swedish chemist Alfred Nobel (1833–1896) had a nitroglycerine factory. Nobel did a great deal of research to try and find a way of making nitroglycerine safer. In 1864, Nobel's factory blew up, killing his brother Emil and several other people. However, Nobel continued his research. In 1867, he found that if the nitroglycerine was mixed with an earthy substance, it became much safer. Nobel called his new, safe explosive "dynamite". It was used for engineering and building work. But, unlike gunpowder, it could not be powdered and used in weapons.

Medical reactions

Chemistry had now become big business in fields other than making soap and explosives. In the 19th century, scientists had discovered the **bacteria** that caused disease. Some chemists now started looking for chemicals that could combat these bacteria, and for drugs that could ease pain.

It had long been known that an extract of willow bark could be used as a painkiller. Then, in 1860, the German chemist Hermann Kolbe (1818–1884) and his students made the sodium salt of salicylic acid in the laboratory. It proved to be a good painkiller, but it often caused stomach upsets.

Easy on the stomach

In 1897, Felix Hoffman (1868–1946), who worked for the German chemical company Bayer, was looking for a painkiller to ease his father's pains from rheumatism (painful, inflamed joints). By adding an acetyl group (—CH_3) to salicylic acid, he produced a drug that was much easier on the stomach than Kolbe's painkiller. The drug was called aspirin.

The green circles are carbon **atoms**, the white are hydrogen, and the red are oxygen.

HOW DOES ASPIRIN WORK?

Aspirin (right) is used to relieve headaches and pain in muscles and joints. It can also reduce fever and inflammation (swelling). Aspirin acts by blocking the production of body chemicals known as prostaglandins. These chemicals are involved in blood clotting, and they also make nerve endings sensitive to pain. By reducing the production of prostaglandins, aspirin reduces the body's sensitivity to pain.

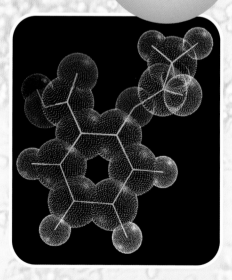

Chemists discovered aspirin by isolating a natural substance that was useful medically. They then made many variants of the substance, in the hope of finding one that worked better than the original. Since that time, other drugs have been found using a similar method.

However, one of Kolbe's students, Paul Ehrlich (1854–1915), found the first **antibiotic** using a different method. He and his assistants tested hundreds of chemicals, including some inorganic substances such as arsenic **compounds**. They were looking for substances that would harm the **microbes** that cause disease but would not harm humans. He found a dye, later named salvarsan, which proved to be very effective against the microbe that causes syphilis (an infectious disease).

Domagk's daughter

In 1932, another German chemist, Gerhard Domagk (1895–1964), also looked at many dyes while he was searching for an antibiotic. He found that a dye called Prontosil worked very well against a range of bacteria. Soon after this discovery, Domagk's young daughter became dangerously ill. At this time Domagk had tested Prontosil in mice, but he did not yet know if it was safe for humans. However, he was desperate to save his daughter, so he treated her with the drug. To his great joy, his daughter made a complete recovery from her illness.

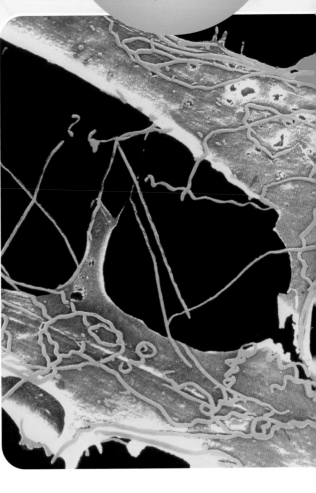

These thin threads are the bacteria that cause syphilis. Syphilis is a sexually transmitted disease that can damage the heart, blood vessels, brain, and spinal cord. Eventually it can cause blindness, insanity, and death.

Drugs from mould

One of the most effective antibiotics was discovered by accident by a Scotsman, Alexander Fleming (1881–1955). Fleming was studying bacteria and other microbes. When he returned from a holiday in 1928, he found that he had left out a dish containing bacteria. The dish had some mould growing on it. Noticing that the areas around the mould were clear of bacteria, Fleming guessed that the mould must be producing some substance that stopped the bacteria from growing.

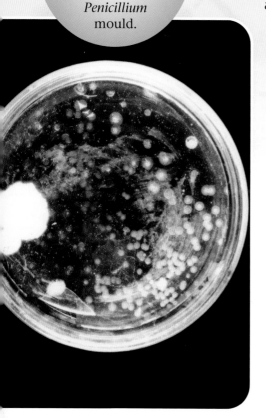

Alexander Fleming took this photograph of his original culture dish containing bacteria and the *Penicillium* mould.

Fleming did many experiments with the mould, which was called *Penicillium notatum*. He was unable to isolate the active substance from the mould, but he did give it a name. He called it penicillin.

Ten years later, in 1938, the Australian Howard Florey (1898–1968) and the German-born biochemist Ernst Chain (1906–1979) took up Fleming's work. Initial tests on mice were very promising, so Florey and Chain enlisted help in the United Kingdom and from the United States to test the drug. By 1941, penicillin was being used to treat soldiers with infected wounds.

HOW DID PENICILLIN SAVE THE COCOANUT GROVE VICTIMS?

In 1942, disaster struck when the Cocoanut Grove nightclub in Boston, in the United States, caught fire. Between 800 and 1,000 people were in the club at the time. Hundreds died in the fire, and many of those who survived were badly burned. At the time, burns victims often died from infections they picked up while they were recovering. However, the Cocoanut Grove victims were treated with penicillin, and nearly all of them survived.

Computers and drugs

In the late 20th century, computers started to play an important part in drug research. Most drugs act by binding to specific sites in the body. The shape of the drug is very important because it has to fit the binding site, just as a key fits a lock. Scientists can use various techniques to work out the shapes of sites where drugs act. Once they know the shape of a site, they can make a computer model showing exactly what the site looks like.

The red circles show the sites where opiate drugs act on our brains. Opiate drugs are excellent painkillers, but they have a bad side-effect – they are addictive. Chemists are using computer modelling to look for alternative painkillers that are not addictive.

Chemists can use the computer model to look for new drugs that have the right shape to fit into a particular site. They can also check the fit of existing drugs with the site. All this can be done on the computer, without making any actual drugs. However, once a potential drug has been found, it still has to be made and tested, to check that it is safe and effective.

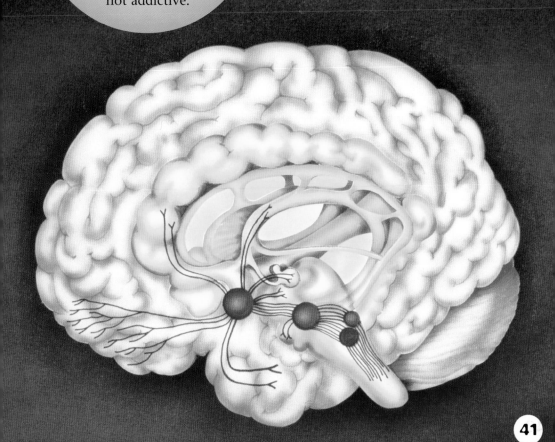

Dividing atoms

By the end of the 19th century, chemists had made enormous progress in understanding chemical reactions. But what was happening at the atomic level? How did particles within **atoms** differ from each other? And how did they join together?

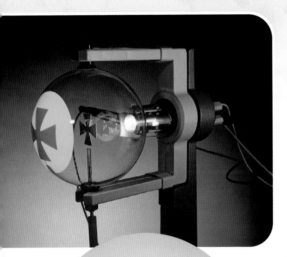

In this vacuum tube, a beam of electrons travels from the cathode (negative electrode) and hits the glass, which glows green. The electrons travel in straight lines, like beams of light. If they did not, the cross would not form a shadow.

The first clues came when chemists started passing electric currents through a **vacuum**. When a glass tube containing a vacuum was hooked up to an electricity supply, it produced a glow of light in the tube. The English chemist William Crookes (1832–1919) showed that the glow was produced by "rays" of electricity that travelled from the negative to the positive **electrode**. In 1897, J.J. Thomson (1856–1940), the English physicist, showed that this electricity was a beam of negatively charged particles, each one nearly 2,000 times lighter than the smallest atom. Since these particles carried electricity, they were called **electrons**.

Strange radiations

The discovery of electrons showed that atoms were not the smallest particles – they were made up of smaller parts. But what was the rest of the atom made of?

It took a long time to find this out. The answer came from studying a strange type of radiation that was discovered in 1896. The French physicist Henri Becquerel (1852–1908) was studying chemicals that glow in the dark. He thought that they might radiate (give out) X-rays. He found that one chemical, which contained uranium, produced a completely different kind of radiation. This radiation was produced all the time – it seemed to be a property of the material itself.

Radioactivity

In 1897, a talented young chemist called Marie Curie (1867–1934) was looking for a subject for her postgraduate studies. She decided to study the unusual radiation that Becquerel had observed. She called it **radioactivity**.

Curie's early studies showed that radioactivity was produced by uranium atoms. However, pitchblende, the most common rock containing uranium, had more radioactivity than could be explained by the uranium in it. Curie was convinced that there must be other radioactive material in pitchblende. She and her husband Pierre worked together, looking for this material. In 1898, they found two new radioactive **elements**. These new elements were polonium and radium.

Marie and Pierre Curie did not have a proper laboratory when they were trying to isolate radium from pitchblende. They worked in a cold, draughty shed.

MARIE CURIE'S STORY

Marie Curie was Polish, but she moved to Paris in 1891 in order to study chemistry. At this time there were strong prejudices against women studying science. Nevertheless, Curie succeeded in becoming the first female professor of science, and the first woman to win a Nobel Prize. In fact she won two Nobel Prizes – one with her husband and Henri Becquerel for explaining radioactivity (1903), and one on her own for discovering radium (1911).

Positive rays

Marie Curie went on to use radium as a treatment for cancer. However, other scientists studied the radiation produced by radioactive elements. There appeared to be three types of radiation. The New Zealand physicist Ernest Rutherford named them alpha, beta, and gamma radiation. It seemed that radioactive atoms were unstable, and threw off bits of themselves. Beta radiation was found to be beams of electrons. Gamma radiation was a type of wave radiation, like X-rays and light. However, alpha rays were something new. They were rays of positively charged particles, and each particle was as heavy as four hydrogen atoms.

Ernest Rutherford is shown here on the right, at the Cavendish Laboratory, Cambridge, in the United Kingdom. Rutherford made many important discoveries about atoms and radioactivity in this laboratory.

Atomic structure

The alpha particles solved the problem of what atoms were made of, besides electrons. Each alpha particle contained two positively charged particles about the weight of a hydrogen atom, and two particles that weighed about the same but had no charge. The charged particles were named **protons**, and the uncharged ones were named **neutrons**.

With the discovery of protons and neutrons, scientists at last understood the structure of atoms. Each atom has a heavy **nucleus**, made of protons and neutrons, surrounded by a cloud of one or more fast-moving, light electrons.

Each element is made of atoms with different numbers of protons and electrons in it. Hydrogen atoms have one proton and one electron. Helium, the next lightest element, has two protons and two electrons (it can also have one or two neutrons). Lithium has three protons and electrons, beryllium has four, and so on.

This diagram shows an atom of beryllium, with four protons, four electrons, and five neutrons. Below it are the nuclei of hydrogen, helium, and carbon. The helium nucleus is the same as a particle of alpha radiation.

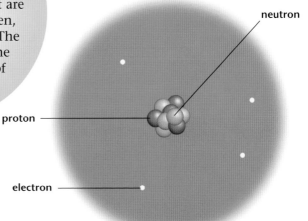

neutron

proton

electron

hydrogen nucleus
(1 proton)

helium nucleus
(2 protons, 2 neutrons)

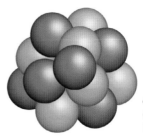

carbon nucleus
(12 protons, 12 neutrons)

THAT'S AMAZING!

Ernest Rutherford and other scientists experimented with firing beams of alpha rays at different materials to see what would happen. Rutherford fired alpha particles at a thin piece of gold foil, and found that most of them went straight through. He concluded that atoms must be mostly empty space. The nucleus of each atom is actually very tiny, while the electron cloud surrounding each nucleus stops the nuclei from getting close to each other. If an atom was the size of a football stadium, the nucleus of the atom would be the size of a pea!

Big molecules

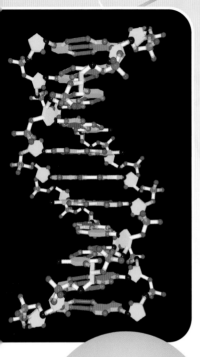

Once they had worked out the structure of **atoms** and **elements**, chemists were able to understand a lot more about chemical reactions. This new understanding helped organic chemists when they began to investigate probably the most complex chemistry of all – the chemistry of life itself.

The first person to look carefully at the chemicals in living cells was Emil Fischer (1852–1919), a German chemist. Fischer discovered nearly all the most important building blocks of life.

Purines, sugars, and proteins

In his early experiments Fischer studied a group of chemicals called the **purines**. These included caffeine (from tea and coffee) and theobromine (found in chocolate). Purines were later found to be an important part of **DNA**.

DNA is made up of two long chains of subunits twisted together in a double spiral. Purines are an important part of about half these subunits.

After working on purines, Fischer began to study sugars. He worked out the structures of common sugars for the first time, and **synthesized** glucose and other sugars. Fischer was also interested in the chemical reactions by which sugars are broken down. He was the first to understand that **enzymes** acted as **catalysts** in these reactions.

HOW WAS THE STRUCTURE OF DNA DISCOVERED?

By the early 1950s, it was clear that purines were an important part of DNA (the material our **genes** are made of). In 1953, James Watson and Francis Crick, at Cambridge University, in the United Kingdom, worked out the DNA molecule's structure. They realized that DNA had a double spiral structure after seeing some X-ray photographs of DNA crystals. These photographs had been taken by Rosalind Franklin, a molecular biologist working at King's College, London.

From about 1899, Fischer began to study proteins. He discovered that proteins were large **molecules** made from smaller building blocks called **amino acids**.

Chains of paper clips

Fischer found many of the chemicals of life, but the scientist who began to fit them together was another German, Hermann Staudinger (1881–1965). In 1910, Staudinger was trying to make isoprene, the basic unit of natural rubber. At that time most organic chemists thought that substances such as rubber, starch, and proteins were loose groupings of small molecules. However, Staudinger was convinced that this was wrong. He thought that these substances were all giant molecules, in which the small molecules were joined together in strings, like chains of paper clips. At first most other scientists rejected Staudinger's ideas. However, evidence for his theory slowly grew, and it gradually began to be accepted. The stage was set for chemists to make giant molecules of their own.

Hermann Staudinger showed that substances such as (a) rubber, (b) starch, and (c) proteins are large molecules made up of chains of smaller subunits.

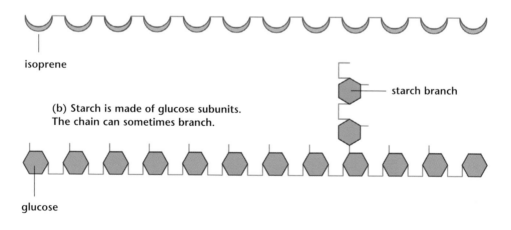

(a) Rubber is made of chains of identical isoprene units.

isoprene

(b) Starch is made of glucose subunits. The chain can sometimes branch.

starch branch

glucose

(c) Proteins are made of different amino acid subunits.

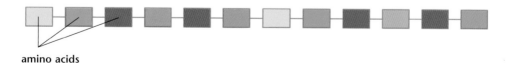

amino acids

Making large molecules

Staudinger coined a name for very large molecules – he called them macromolecules. Chemists were soon taking Staudinger's ideas about these natural macromolecules and using them to make completely new materials, called plastics.

Plastics are also known as polymers ("poly" means "many"). They are chains of many small molecules (monomers) joined together.

Some types of plastic had already been made from natural polymers. In the 19th century, chemists developed processes for extracting cellulose from wood. Cellulose is a natural polymer made from long chains of sugars. The extracted cellulose was made into a fibre known as rayon and the plastic celluloid. The best-known use for celluloid was for making film for cameras.

Another early plastic was casein, made in the 1890s from soured milk and methanal (formaldehyde). Casein was used to make buttons and billiard balls. A third plastic, Bakelite, could be moulded and then set to form a hard plastic. Bakelite was invented by the Belgian-born American chemist Leo Baekeland (1863–1944) in 1909.

This 1950s radio was made from Bakelite. Before he developed Bakelite, Baekeland invented the first successful film material, which he called Velox.

Plastics from oil

Early plastics were made from a range of materials. Then, in the 1920s, an American chemist discovered something that made petroleum (oil) the starting point for most plastics. Crude petroleum consists of hydrocarbons. These are **compounds** made from carbon and hydrogen, in which the carbons are joined together in long chains. George Curme (1888–1976) found a way of "cracking" petroleum at high temperatures and pressures, to break up these chains into smaller, more reactive molecules. These molecules turned out to be ideal for making plastics.

By the late 1920s, chemists understood how to make polymers, and knew that they could be very useful materials. Chemists then began to try to make plastics with specific properties. In the United States, in 1926, Waldo Semon developed a form of the plastic polyvinyl chloride (PVC) that could be moulded easily. In the early 1930s, Wallace Carothers succeeded in developing a **synthetic** rubber (neoprene) and a plastic fibre called nylon, which could be woven into a fine material similar to silk.

Nylon was immediately successful because it was used to make cheaper, hard-wearing replacements for silk stockings. The new stockings soon became known as nylons. In their first day on sale, 5 million pairs of nylons were sold.

THAT'S AMAZING!

In the 1860s, a form of cellulose called celluloid was made in the United States by John Wesley Hyatt. Celluloid was used to make film, artificial legs, dentures, and billiard balls, among other things. However, celluloid was made from cellulose nitrate, a close relation of nitrocellulose or guncotton (see page 37). Most of the time it was stable, but occasionally billiard balls exploded when they hit each other, and films suddenly caught fire!

The plastics boom

During the Second World War (1939–1945), many new plastics were developed. Then, in the 1950s and 1960s, plastics began to replace traditional materials in a huge range of products. Many household objects were made of plastic, and clothes were made from synthetic fabrics such as nylon and rayon.

The plastic PTFE (Teflon®) was used as a non-stick coating for pans, but also for coating all types of joints that needed lubricating. Other less obvious materials, such as paints, polishes, and adhesives, were also made from plastics.

Plastic batteries

One area in which plastics have not yet replaced other materials is in electrical wiring and electronic parts. However, this could soon change. In the 1970s, a Japanese chemistry student was trying to make a plastic called polyacetylene, but he added too much of the catalyst that makes the reaction happen. He ended up producing a film of silvery, metallic-looking material.

American scientist Alan MacDiarmid thought that this material might conduct electricity, and began experimenting with it. The result was a range of plastics that can conduct electricity, and others that can act as semiconductors (the materials used for making electronic devices). Batteries and electronic devices have been developed from these new materials. Plastic batteries are cheap and flexible, but not yet as powerful as conventional batteries.

WHAT IS KEVLAR®?

In 1965, Stephanie Kwolek, working for DuPont Chemicals in the United States, discovered a new type of polymer that was very stiff and strong, and did not melt at high temperatures. After several years of experimenting, this discovery led to the production of Kevlar®. This was a material strong enough to be used in aircraft bodies, bullet-proof vests, tyres, bicycle frames, and sports equipment.

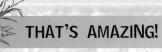

In the 1980s, English chemist Harold Kroto was studying chains of carbon atoms that had been detected in space. He teamed up with two researchers in the United States, Richard Smalley and Robert Curl, to investigate how these carbon chains might be made. They experimented with vaporizing graphite (a form of pure carbon) in a helium atmosphere. The results were a surprise. As well as the carbon chains they had been hoping to make, the researchers had created a completely new form of carbon – a molecule that was made up of 60 to 600 carbon atoms, arranged in hexagons and pentagons like the patches on a football. These molecules were called Buckminster fullerenes, and they are usually known as fullerenes or buckyballs. Richard Smalley went on to produce related carbon molecules that were tube-shaped. These **nanotubes** can be made into fibres that are stronger than a spider's silk.

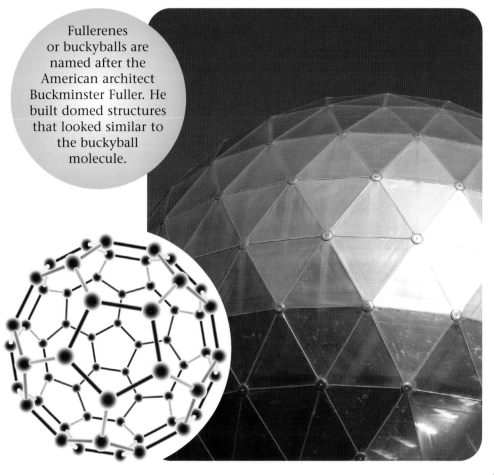

Fullerenes or buckyballs are named after the American architect Buckminster Fuller. He built domed structures that looked similar to the buckyball molecule.

From gunpowder to lasers

Today, chemists can do amazing things with chemical reactions. Huge chemical factories and petroleum refineries produce the raw materials for all types of everyday materials, from plastics to perfumes. Unfortunately, some of the waste materials produced by these factories have been shown to be bad for the environment, and this has been causing increasing concern. Scientists have therefore been looking for ways to control reactions more carefully, to avoid producing waste that can pollute the water and air.

Living catalysts

One new method of controlling reactions involves **enzymes**, the **catalysts** used by living things. Reactions that use enzymes have several advantages. They happen at normal temperatures and pressures, whereas industrial chemistry often involves high temperatures and pressures. In this way, using enzymes can reduce the need for energy to heat or pressurize substances.

Enzymes are also very specific: they make one particular reaction happen, and not others. In industrial chemistry the product that is wanted is often one of several produced, and other products have to be thrown away as waste.

HOW ARE ENZYMES USED?

Enzymes are used in many different ways, for instance to make biological washing powders, baby foods, sports drinks, foods for slimmers, and soft-centred chocolates. More recently, chemists have found ways to use **microbes** to produce large quantities of specific enzymes. **Genes** from humans or other living things are artificially inserted into the microbes to make them produce useful substances such as medicines, basic chemicals, plastics, and other materials.

Laser chemistry

In the future, chemical reactions may be controlled with lasers. Chemists know that **atoms** or **molecules** react when they become energized or excited. Chemists have also found that different amounts of energy are needed to excite different materials. Researchers are experimenting with ways of using lasers to supply just the right amount of energy to make one reaction happen, but not another. This research is still in its early stages, but it has already been possible to make some simple reactions happen this way.

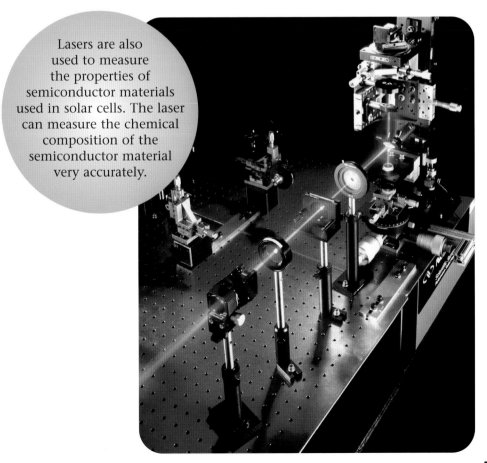

Lasers are also used to measure the properties of semiconductor materials used in solar cells. The laser can measure the chemical composition of the semiconductor material very accurately.

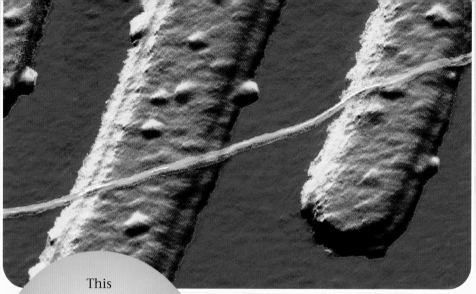

This photograph, taken with a special microscope and magnified 120,000 times, shows a nanotube (the thin blue line). The "wires" of a modern microchip (yellow) look huge and clumsy in comparison.

Following the chain

We have followed the chain of important discoveries from gunpowder to laser chemistry. So, what next? Some new areas of chemistry are growing rapidly, and may soon become as common as computers. For instance, "smart" materials that can change their properties to suit their environment are already being developed. Shape-change metals can "remember" a particular shape and return to it when they are heated. There are also liquids that solidify when an electric current is passed through them. **Nanotubes** (see page 51) promise to be important in the future. Laser chemistry could give chemists more control over reactions than they have ever had before. The story of chemical reactions goes on.

THAT'S AMAZING!

Nanotubes could one day be as important as plastics are now. At the moment, there are some problems still to be solved. However, in the near future they could be used to make super-small computers and electronic devices, such as fuel cells that produce electricity from hydrogen. They could also be used to produce materials that are stronger than the most advanced modern **composites**, and to make parts in microscopic machines.

What have we found out?

Chemists before Lavoisier showed that the air is a mixture of gases, mainly nitrogen and oxygen. In the 18th century, Lavoisier showed that fire is not an **element**, but a chemical reaction that relies on oxygen to work. Then Dalton explained that chemical reactions are rearrangements of the atoms that make up all materials.

The work of chemists, such as Berzelius and Davy, showed that electricity was involved in chemical reactions, and that chemical reactions could be used to make electricity. However, it took another 100 years to understand how electricity was involved. During that time, chemists gained knowledge of organic reactions, and developed industrial processes for making some chemicals.

Eventually the work of Curie, Rutherford, and others showed that atoms were made from a mixture of particles, some of which were electrically charged. Chemists now understood the differences between elements. They also realized that chemical reactions happened between the **electrons** of atoms, and did not involve the **nucleus**.

More than 2,000 years ago, the Chinese used gunpowder to make fireworks. However, they did not understand the chemical reactions that made the gunpowder ignite, and the rockets fly.

In the 20th century, chemists began to understand the reactions that go on in living things. They also used chemical reactions to make drugs, plastics, and a wide range of other new materials. Now, in the 21st century, chemists are using lasers to look at what happens, moment by moment, in chemical reactions, including **combustion**. Laser chemistry promises to give us far greater control over chemical reactions in the future.

Timeline

800 BC Earliest records of alchemists in China.

9th century AD Gunpowder first made in China.

13th century Secret of making gunpowder reaches Europe via Arab alchemists.

1659 Robert Boyle shows that air is needed both for combustion and for respiration (breathing).

1668 John Mayow shows that only a particular part of the air is needed for combustion.

early 18th century Georg Stahl develops the phlogiston theory.

1756 Joseph Black publishes his discovery of carbon dioxide.

1766 Henry Cavendish discovers the element hydrogen.

1774 Joseph Priestley discovers oxygen, but calls it "dephlogisticated air".

1775–1780 Antoine Lavoisier names oxygen and shows how it is involved in combustion.

1790 Nicolas Leblanc develops a process to make soda ash.

1792 Jeremias Richter shows that the amount of acid needed to neutralize a particular base is the same every time.

1798 Count Rumford suggests that heat is energy.

1799 Humphry Davy discovers properties of laughing gas (nitrous oxide).

1803 John Dalton explains his theory of atomic weights.

1803 Jöns Berzelius uses a battery for electrolysis.

1807 Davy uses electrolysis to discover the elements sodium and potassium.

1811 Berzelius devises system of chemical symbols.

1826 Berzelius publishes tables of over 2,000 atomic weights.

1828 Friedrich Wöhler succeeds in synthesizing urea.

1833 Michael Faraday suggests how electrolysis works.

1850s Marcellin Berthelot synthesizes many organic chemicals.

1852 Edward Frankland suggests theory of valency (combining power).

1856 William Perkin makes mauveine, the first synthetic dye.

1858 Auguste Kekulé shows that carbon forms four bonds and that carbon atoms can link together in chains.

1860s Berthelot builds a bomb calorimeter for measuring heat changes that occur in chemical reactions.

1860s Solvay process is developed for making soda ash.

1867 Alfred Nobel invents dynamite.

1890s Plastic casein made from soured milk and methanal.

1891 Sir James Dewar and Frederick Abel develop cordite, which replaces gunpowder in guns.

1894 Emil Fischer synthesizes natural sugars.

1896 Henri Becquerel discovers a new type of radiation.

1897 Industrial process is developed for making indigo dye.

1897 J.J. Thomson discovers electrons in the nucleus of an atom.

1897 Felix Hoffman synthesizes the painkiller aspirin.

1898 Marie and Pierre Curie discover polonium and radium.

1907 Fischer synthesizes a small protein chain.

1909 Fritz Haber develops large-scale process for making ammonia from nitrogen and hydrogen.

1909 Leo Baekeland synthesizes the plastic Bakelite.

1909 Paul Ehrlich develops the drug salvarsan.

1920s George Curme discovers how to "crack" petroleum.

1922 Hermann Staudinger and J. Fritschi propose that proteins are giant molecules.

1926 Waldo Semon develops the plastic PVC.

1928 Alexander Fleming finds that *Penicillium* mould can destroy bacteria.

1932 Gerhard Domagk synthesizes Prontosil, one of the first antibiotics.

1934 Wallace Carothers and his team develop nylon.

1941 Howard Florey and Ernst Chain develop penicillin.

1953 Francis Crick and James Watson discover the structure of DNA.

1965 Stephanie Kwolek discovers the plastic Kevlar®.

1977 Hideki Shirakawa, Alan MacDiarmid, and Alan J. Heeger develop plastics that are able to conduct electricity.

1985 Harold Kroto, Richard Smalley, and Robert Curl synthesize Buckminster fullerenes.

2005 Richard Mathies and his colleagues at the University of California, in the United States, use lasers to film a chemical reaction.

Biographies

These are some of the leading scientists in the story of chemistry.

Jöns Berzelius (1779–1848)

Berzelius was born in Sorgard, Sweden. He was one of the great chemists of his time. He is most famous for producing the first accurate atomic weights, for inventing the system of chemical symbols, and for his work on electrolysis. Berzelius's father died when Berzelius was still young. At the age of 12, Berzelius was sent away to school, where he proved to be very good at languages. He was apprenticed to a pharmacist and a doctor before going on to study at university. As well as his own research, Berzelius is famous for teaching many students who went on to become important chemists in their own right.

Robert Boyle (1627–1691)

Irishman Robert Boyle was one of 14 children. His father was the wealthiest man in Britain at the time. Boyle studied at Eton public school and then with private tutors. From 1656 to 1668 he lived and worked in Oxford, where he did many of the experiments that made him famous. As well as his experiments on burning and breathing with Robert Hooke, Boyle was famous for his law stating the relationship between the pressure and volume of a gas.

Ernst Chain (1906–1979) and Howard Florey (1898–1968)

German Ernst Chain and Australian Howard Florey together developed the drug penicillin between 1939 and 1941. After studying in Australia, Florey moved to Oxford, in the United Kingdom, in 1936. Chain studied chemistry in Berlin, Germany, but then moved first to Cambridge and then to Oxford, where he began working with Florey. In addition to his work on antibiotics, Chain worked on snake venoms and on insulin.

Francis Crick (1916–2004) and James Watson (1928–)

Francis Crick was born in Northampton, in the United Kingdom, while James Watson was from Chicago, in the United States. Crick first studied physics, but after the Second World War (1939–1945) he turned to biology. Watson was a keen bird-watcher as a boy, which led him to study zoology and genetics. Watson and Crick met up in 1951 at the Cavendish Laboratory, at Cambridge University, in the United Kingdom. They worked together on the structure of DNA, which they discovered in 1953. Crick did important work on how DNA acts in cells, then moved into brain research. Watson still works in DNA research.

Marie Curie (1867–1934)

Marie Curie was called Manya Sklodowska when she was born in Poland, but later became a French citizen. After working to help her sister study medicine in Paris, France, Marie herself went to Paris and studied physics and chemistry. In 1895, she married Pierre Curie. Together, Marie and Pierre studied radioactivity and carried out the work that led to the discovery of radium. Pierre died in an accident in 1906, but Marie continued to work on radioactivity and, later, X-rays. Her daughter Irene was also a famous scientist.

John Dalton (1766–1844)

John Dalton was brought up in Cumbria, in the north of England. By the time he was 12, he was helping to teach at his school in Kendal. He stayed there for 10 years before taking another teaching job in Manchester. Dalton became famous for his atomic theory and tables of atomic weights, but he was also fascinated by the weather. He kept a daily record of weather conditions from 1787 until the day of his death.

Humphry Davy (1778–1829)

Humphry Davy was an English chemist, famous for discovering several elements and for his work on electrolysis. He also invented the miner's safety lamp. Davy was born and went to school in Cornwall. In 1798 he worked at the Pneumatic Institute in Bristol, where he discovered nitrous oxide (laughing gas). In 1801 he was invited to lecture at the Royal Institution in London. His lectures were very popular, and he did his most important research there.

Harry Kroto (1939–)

Englishman Harry Kroto is famous for his discovery of a completely new form of carbon called Buckminster fullerene. At school Kroto was a promising artist, but he later became interested in chemistry. After university he worked in Canada for a time, then in 1967 became Professor of Chemistry at Sussex University, in the United Kingdom. While he was at Sussex he began the research that led him to work with Americans Richard Smalley and Robert Curl and eventually to their synthesis of the Buckminster fullerene carbon molecule.

Antoine Lavoisier (1743–1794)

Antoine Lavoisier lived most of his life in Paris, France. At university he studied law, but he also went to many lectures on chemistry and physics. After college he invested in a profitable business that involved collecting taxes. This gave him the time and money to study chemistry rather than becoming a lawyer. In 1771 he married Marie Anne Paulze, who soon became an important assistant in his research. Lavoisier is often called the "father of chemistry". He provided a scientific basis for chemistry, using careful experiments and accurate measurements to test and prove his ideas.

Glossary

acid substance that turns litmus paper red and neutralizes alkalis

alkali substance that turns litmus paper blue and neutralizes acids

amino acid one of 20 different, related chemicals that are the building blocks of proteins

antibiotic medicine that can kill bacteria and other microbes (but not viruses)

atom extremely tiny particle that forms the basic building block of all substances

atomic weight weight of an atom of an element relative to the weight of another element that is used as a standard. Modern atomic weights are measured relative to carbon, which is given an atomic weight of 12.

bacterium microscopic living thing made up of a single cell with a simple structure. Some bacteria can cause disease.

base alkali that is not dissolved in water

catalyst substance that speeds up a chemical reaction, but remains itself unchanged by the reaction

combustion chemical reaction of burning

composite solid material that is made up of two or more different substances

compound substance that is made up of molecules

DNA chemical, found in every living cell, that carries all the cell's basic life instructions

electrode one of the poles of a battery or electric cell

electrolysis chemical reaction produced by passing electricity through a substance or mixture

electron tiny, negatively charged particle that forms part of an atom

element substance made up of just one type of atom

endothermic (of a chemical reaction) taking in heat

enzyme protein that speeds up a chemical reaction in a living thing

exothermic (of a chemical reaction) giving out heat

gene section of DNA that gives a particular characteristic to a living thing

inflammable possible to burn

ion atom that has an electrical charge

microbe microscopic living thing

molecule group of atoms that are joined together chemically

nanotube microscopic tube-shaped molecule made of pure carbon

neutron tiny particle with no electric charge found in the nucleus of an atom

nucleus central part of an atom; plural "nuclei"

ore rock that contains a metal in its natural state

oxidation chemical reaction in which oxygen is incorporated into a substance

phlogiston substance that 17th-century scientists thought was given off when something was burning

pigment coloured chemical found, for example, in dyes

proton tiny particle with a positive electric charge found in the nucleus of an atom

purine substance found in living things, including caffeine (found in tea and coffee) and theobromine (found in chocolate)

radioactivity radiation from the nucleus of an atom

solution liquid that has a solid or gas mixed into it

synthesize make in a laboratory

synthetic made in a laboratory

thermodynamics study of the changes in heat or other energy during a chemical reaction or other process

vacuum emptiness; what is left when air is pumped out of a flask or other container

valency combining power of an element: how many other atoms it can join with

Further resources

If you have enjoyed this book and want to find out more, you can look at the following books and websites.

Books

The Chemical History of a Candle
Michael Faraday
(Dover, New York, 2002)

Chemical Reactions
Carol Baldwin
(Raintree, 2006)

Horrible Science: Chemical Chaos
Nick Arnold
(Scholastic Hippo, 2005)

Pioneers in Science: Chemistry
Katherine Cullen, Scott McCutcheon, and Bobbi McCutcheon
(Facts on File, 2006)

The Search for Radium: Marie Curie's Story
Christian Birmingham
(Matthew Price, 2004)

Websites

Chemistry: A Historical Perspective
www.3rd1000.com/history/contents.htm.
An excellent history of chemistry.

The Chemical Elements
http://homepage.mac.com/dtrapp/Elements/elements.html
Find out how every chemical element was named and discovered on this interesting website.

Chemistry Timeline
www.psigate.ac.uk/newsite/chemistry_timeline.html
Important events in chemistry since 10,000 BC.

Distinguished Women
www.distinguishedwomen.com/subject/chem.html
Information about Marie Curie and other women who have contributed to chemistry.

The Future's Plastic
www.bbc.co.uk/radio4/science/futuresplastic.shtml
Listen to two radio programmes on the history of plastic from BBC Radio 4.

The Nobel Prize
http://nobelprize.org/nobel/
This site has information on every Nobel Prize winner since the prize was first awarded. Many winners have written autobiographies.

Pharmaceutical Achievers
www.chemheritage.org/EducationalServices/pharm/pa/home.htm
This website about some of the important drug discoveries of the 20th century has some good stories about Fleming, Domagk, Florey, Chain, and several other scientists.

Index

Titles in the *Chain Reactions* series include:

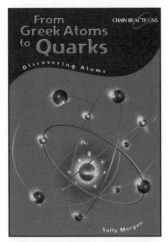

Hardback 978 0 431 18657 3

Hardback 978 0 431 18658 0

Hardback 978 0 431 18659 7

Hardback 978 0 431 18660 3

Hardback 978 0 431 18661 0

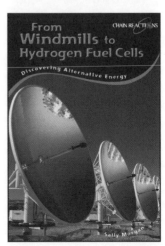

Hardback 978 0 431 18662 7

Find out about other titles from Heinemann Library on our website www.heinemann.co.uk/library